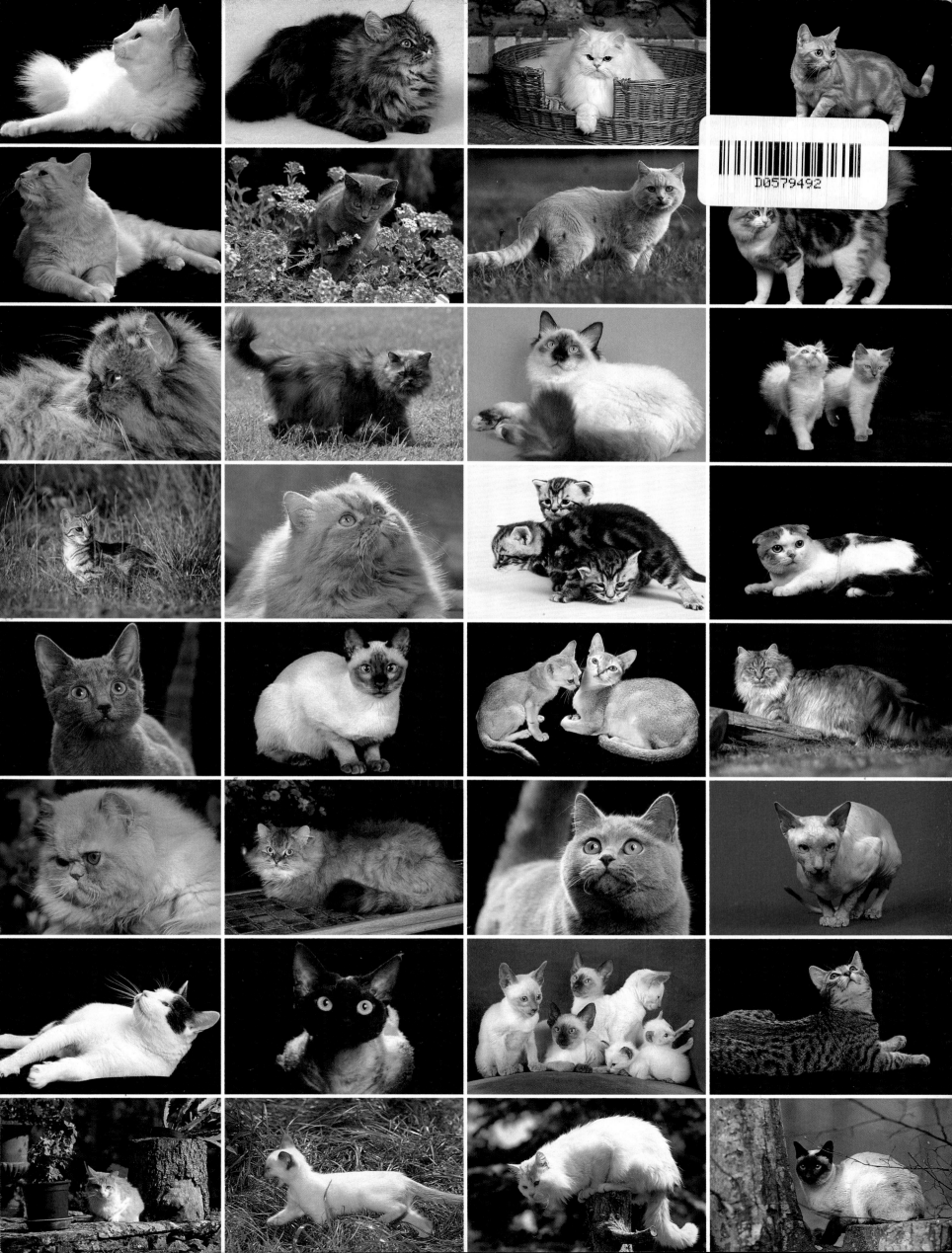

# 1001
## IMAGES OF
# CATS

TEXT BY PHILIPPE COPPÉ

**TIGER BOOKS INTERNATIONAL**
**LONDON**

# CONTENTS

3221
This edition published in 1992 by Tiger Books International PLC, London
© 1992 Colour Library Books Ltd, Godalming, Surrey
Printed and bound in Spain
All rights reserved
ISBN 1 85501 287 1

# FOREWORD

The photogenic quality of the cat is not a new phenomenon nor is it likely to fade: cats, big and small alike, are amongst the favourite subjects of photographers. Perhaps this is because cats take a mischievous delight in posing for the camera. Perhaps it is simply because there is no end to the fascination the animal holds for those who love it. The varying, rich colours of its coat, its air of mystery, its ability to look detached or astonished, its penetrating gaze and almost mystical serenity all make it a great model for amateur and professional photographer alike. The cat lives on several planes: the carefree pussy cat, languidly stretched out in a luxurious setting; the intelligent cat, with eyes half closed, seated between a desk lamp and a typewriter, and the streetwise tom cat, free but scarred by life.

There are many sides to the cat, and asleep, at play, hunting or just amusing us, it makes endless lovely pictures.

Which is why this is, first and foremost, a picture book – with a short, explanatory text. So much has been written about the cat but it still remains an enigma – no one knows better than a true cat lover that its secrets are impenetrable.

You will be able to study the cat a thousand times in the pages of this book. A thousand photographs cover every breed: common, classic or unusual, from the hairiest to the hairless, from the plainest to the prettiest: they are all here.

Designed so that the reader may discover his or her favourite at a glance, this book is for both the knowledgable cat lover and the newcomer to cats – who may not know the great variety of creatures which hide behind the name "cat": like the Abyssinian, Angora, Somali, Persian, Siamese, Ocicat, British Shorthair, Scottish Fold, Japanese Bobtail, Exotic Shorthair, Burmese, Devon Rex, to name just a few at random. White, grey, cream, ginger, brown, chocolate or black, short haired, curly coated, medium long or long haired; the permutations are endless.

And when you close this book we hope that as well as having had an opportunity to enjoy looking at all these wonderful creatures, you will also have learnt something of their enchanting character and fascinating behaviour.

# SHORTHAIR CATS

# ABYSSINIAN

There is a well known story told about an Englishwoman who longed to possess a pure bred Abyssinian. Mrs Forbes, just after the First World War, actually journeyed to Ethiopia and travelled through the country in peril of life and limb, looking for the perfect specimen – which of course she did not find as the Abyssinian is an English breed, which was introduced in London in 1868!

In fact, this little feline, often described as the archetypal cat, is of African descent. A British diplomat, posted to Addis Abbaba, fell in love with one of his Ethiopian friend's cats. The animal possessed a very interesting coat, the hairs of which were ticked, rather like those of a hare.

When the diplomat was recalled to London he was able to bring the cat back with him, and it proved so popular that he determined to try and reproduce it. After a number of failures he finally succeeded in breeding a litter of kittens with ticked coats. Breeders of Abyssinians had to fight for years to get the breed recognised. It was only in 1929 that the Governing Council of the Cat Fancy decided to admit the Abyssinian to the holiest of holies.

Since then the Abyssinian has held a place in the first rank of feline aristocracy. It has become one of the great breeds and is more and more sought after, in both Europe and North America. Its popularity is due not only to its physical appearance but equally to its intellectual and spiritual qualities.

Both in repose and movement, the Abyssinian is always supremely elegant. No other cat can so successfully adopt a hieratical pose. It reminds us of the ancient Egyptian Cat gods, seen on temple columns.

The sight of this cat moving in perfect harmony, the muscles rippling under its skin, with its great expressive eyes, long, pricked up ears and inner air of nobility, makes one see why people fall in love with this perfect animal.

The Abyssinian also makes it easy to understand why the Egyptians revered Bastet, the cat-headed goddess.

Breeders produce Abyssinians of various colours. The most popular is a reddish brown. Standards vary and the following is for the normal ticked, ruddy brown Abyssinian:

## General

Medium sized, long and slender body. Well muscled, supple and extremely well proportioned. Fine, sensitive legs, small feet with black pads. Thick haired, tapering tail.

## Head

Long, delicate and triangular in shape but not exaggeratedly so. The nose is outlined in black. Wide based ears, sometimes with a little tuft of hair at the point, like a lynx. The luminous, almond shaped eyes, outlined in black, are full of expression.

# ABYSSINIAN (cont'd)

Very clean, an excellent climber, and of unequalled robustness, the Abyssinian needs exercise. But it will get used to living in an apartment as long as it is free to move about from one room to another. A terrace or courtyard garden is sufficient for the cat to stretch its legs if necessary. Not inclined to wander, it will not want to go much further.

A proud cat, aware of its strength, the Abyssinian also knows when to give in; it is a one person cat and will give its owner exclusive devotion and obedience.

But with other people the Abyssinian knows what is due to its pride. If you tease it or try too hard to get a response it will quietly withdraw. The claws only ever come out as a last resort.

The Abyssinian is an energetic cat. It needs space. Even in an apartment it will jump from one piece of furniture to another, and it often jumps on top of a high cupboard so it can look down on the world.

If it has the use of a garden, it will be seen climbing trees and even leaping from branch to branch.

The Abyssinian will eat most things, but starchy foods or fatty meats should be excluded from its diet. A mixture of fresh and tinned food should be fed.

Grooming poses no problems. A brush over every two or three days is sufficient. When moulting, a good brushing against the lie of the hair is beneficial.

## Coat

Soft to the touch, it should have no strong markings such as stripes or patches. The ticking, however, must be visible. The fine ticked coat is unique among cats. Each hair has two or three distinct bands of colour, the whole blending into an effect often compared to a Belgian hare. Preferred colouring is reddish brown (known as ruddy in the United States) ticked with black or dark brown. Insides of the legs and the belly should harmonise with the main colour, shades from apricot to dark orange being preferred.

The Red Abyssinian should also have clear ticking, but the colour should be a dark reddish brown throughout, with pink nose and pads.

# AMERICAN CURL

The Scottish Fold cat, with its ears folded flat, has been known for some time and there is now also the American Curl, whose ears turn back at the top to form a crescent shape. The breed was introduced in 1981 at Lakewood, California, by Joe and Grace Luga, who had noticed nothing strange about the ears of their cat until she produced a litter of kittens with curled back ears. By breeding from litter brother and sister the American Curl breed was gradually established. In 1986 it finally became recognised.

This new member of the cat aristocracy soon travelled to Europe and there are now a number of European breeders. Probably the breed would spread even more rapidly if its rarity did not make it so expensive; worth its weight in silver if not gold!

The American curl is an extremely intelligent animal, more intelligent even than many other cats – at least so claim its admirers. A happy cat, it loves to go out and about, overcome obstacles and solve new problems. It can be cunning but the turned back ears sometimes make it look more mischievious than it really is.

Very affectionate, it loves to be picked up or sit on your knee, and it always gives warning before the claws come out.

The Curl needs brushing two or three times a week. Weekly checking over and a carefully weighed and varied diet served at regular times every day will keep it healthy.

## General

Medium but solid bone structure, light weight with medium size feet and paws. The tail is the same length as the body and fairly fluffy.

## Head

A straight, slightly turned up nose. Firm, regular chin. Medium size ears which are turned back over the top of the skull, placed high on the head and well apart. Eyes set in a rounded oval. Their colour may vary except in the Siamese type, where they must be green.

## Coat

Silky with no undercoat. Medium length. There is also a short haired American Curl.

11

# AMERICAN SHORTHAIR, AMERICAN WIREHAIR

Originally the **American Shorthair** was an ordinary domestic cat of no particular breeding which was modified and improved by enthusiasts. And, since the Americans are known never to do anything by halves, in the process they produced a vast number of varieties!

The European cat travelled to America on the Mayflower with the first immigrants, but it had to wait three centuries for recognition. Today the American Shorthair still retains the overall look of its moggy ancestors.

It has also retained their qualities of intelligence, willingness to please and affection for its owners. Here is a cat that is both dependant and independant. Of course it is an excellent mouser.

A hardy cat, resistant to disease, it is easy to look after and to feed.

One day, on a farm in Verona in the State of New York, two kittens in a litter were born with frizzy coats. On becoming adult one of them was crossed with a female of similar coat and so, in 1966, began the line known as the **American Wirehair.** The breed has since become recognised.

Reminiscent of the Rex, the coat is, however, frizzy, as distinct from the curly undercoat of the latter. The hair is much rougher to the touch.

With an apparently more diverse character than the American Shorthair, the agile Wirehair pokes its nose into everything. While affectionate with its master it knows how to make itself respected by other pets or farm animals. It, too, is an excellent mouser.

It only needs an occasional light brush. Not difficult to look after, the Wirehair will eat anything it is given but likes meat best.

9

10

12

## AMERICAN SHORTHAIR
### General
Muscular and solid body firmly planted on moderately long, heavy paws. The medium long tail is ringed and thickly covered in hair.

### Head
Fairly large, with rounded ears set on the top. The eye colour is in harmony with that of the coat.

### Coat
Short, thick hair, covering the whole body, protects it from the cold. They come in a great variety of colours, new ones appearing all the time. These include black, white, grey, blue grey, reddish brown, cream, golden, cameo, black smoke, cameo smoke, tabby, blue smoke, marmalade etc.
The American Shorthair is not well known in Europe, its equivalent being the British Shorthair and the common European cat.
**Photos: 1, 2, 3, 4, 6, 9, 10, 11, 14**

## AMERICAN WIREHAIR
### General
Medium sized, well proportioned, stocky and muscular. The female is smaller than the male. The long tail tapers at the end.

11

13

14

15

### Head
Round shaped with full cheeks, slightly protruding nose and small ears. Extremely bright eyes which match the colour of the coat.

### Coat
Frizzy, medium long haired. Colours vary enormously.
**Photos: 5, 7, 8, 12, 13 & 15**

# RUSSIAN BLUE

No one could call this a nameless cat! It has been known successively as the Maltese Cat, the Blue Archangel, the American Blue, the Spanish Blue and the Archangel Cat. Today it is called – definitively it would seem – the Russian Blue.

Old Russian tales often mention a blue cat which was supposed to bring luck to the home, and an English writer in 1902 claimed that the Russians bred these cats for their fur. "The cats brought by caravans make us realise the large number of blue cats which come from Russia … from the Asian part. Many of the beautiful furs which come out of Russia are in fact cat skins!"

The Russian Blue, as we know it today, was never sacrificed to this trade. It is believed that sailors trading between Russia and the Mediterranean countries brought them by ship, leaving them at Archangel, where they founded a line. Later on their descendants were to be transported in their turn from the Russian port to England, where breeders made them what they are today: wonderful cats with magnificent, emerald green eyes and fur of a unique texture, very thick and soft at the same time, close lying but lovely to touch.

The Russian Blue has royal connections. It was a favoured pet of the Russian Czars, and Queen Victoria had two, which are said to have come directly from the Russian court.

However, establishing the Russian Blue as a breed was not easy. It could be confused with the British blue from one side of the Channel and the Chartreuse from the other. In the end it was decided to create two categories: British Blues and Foreign Blues. At the end of the Second World War an English breeder, Mrs Mary Rochford, decided to take up the Russian Blue and propagate the breed. The standard operating in 1930 was readopted, and in 1967 the Russian Blue Association was founded. Throughout the world, breeders who wish to breed true Russian Blues conform to the standards laid down by this society.

It is good to record that for the true Russian Blue both parents must be of pure blood .The great problem for breeders is that pure bred stud males are hard to find.

If it were possible to class cats by the beauty of their eyes, the Russian Blue would certainly be among the leaders. At shows their deep, shining eyes gaze into those of visitors. Russian Blue kittens are all born with

## General

Long bodied with medium bone structure. Long, slim legs and small, oval feet. Long, straight tail, tapering at the end.

## Head

Fairly wide face with a flat skull. Large, pointed ears, whose skin is transparent. Beautiful luminous green eyes.

## Coat

Short, thick fur, soft and lovely to touch. The undercoat gives it a double thickness and its silvery appearance. The coat must be absolutely unmarked, not a single stripe or patch or spot of colour, only the uniform self colour, which may be any shade of blue or blue grey, is permitted.

# RUSSIAN BLUE
# (cont'd)

blue eyes, which gradually change with maturity to the true green required by the breed standard.

An animal of many attractive qualities, it is tranquil, intelligent, serene, gentle, affectionate, courageous, clean and easy to look after. Generally it is a silent cat and is said to talk with its eyes and its body language. Even when in season, the female only emits a delicate miaow. The Russian Blue makes a great companion, with the slight reservation that it prefers to keep its

distance from strangers. Probably because it is by nature calm, it hates noise, shouting or fuss.

The coat of the Russian Blue should not be flat and it should never be brushed hard or smoothed down. Its diet should be as varied as possible, served at regular times every day, and it should not be overfed.

At home in an apartment, the Russian Blue never has the urge to wander, but it likes to have the freedom to go from room to room. Male and female form a couple and both look after the kittens.

Little attempt has been made to create different varieties of the breed but the English do also breed white Russian Blues and black Russian Blues!

# JAPANESE BOBTAIL

**B**obtails have existed in Japan for centuries and are known there as "chrysanthemum cats" on account of their little stumps of tails which, round and fluffy, appear to open like a chrysanthemum.

This cat has featured in many tales. Commonly known as Mi-ke, in the guise of Mike-Nako, it became the protector of mariners. Climbing the ship's mast, it would put to flight evil genies and the wandering souls of shipwrecked sailors. But it could also transform itself into an evil cat, such as the ogre Neko-Baké, or the two-tailed Neko-Mata.

Originally the Bobtail was always single coloured: white, ginger or black. Colour crosses were developed and today the most sought after is in fact the tricolour

Bobtail. The Bobtail left its homeland during the American occupation of Japan. A breeder, Mrs Judy Crawford, travelled to Japan, patiently studied the breed and, from 1968 onward, exported thirty-eight Bobtails to the United States, where they were much admired.

In Europe the Japanese Bobtail is still very rare. They are difficult to find and extremely expensive if you succeed.

The breed has two peculiarities: its pom pom-shaped stump of a tail and its back end, which slopes in a strange manner. A cat of great character, it is calm, affectionate and usually quiet, but can, when it wants to, produce a noisy miaow which it modifies according to the circumstances. Completely at home with humans it shows total indifference, to the point of disdain, when faced with other animals.

Otherwise, it is interested in everything. Given the opportunity it will climb trees or go hunting. It likes the open air but will live a shut-in existence quite happily.

A gourmet cat, it likes fresh fish best, which should be fed alternately with meat meals. It has a healthy appetite

and therefore needs watching so it does not overeat. Extremely clean, it washes conscientiously. It helps if you give it a light brush every day. Generally healthy it needs to avoid real cold.

## General

Medium sized body, supple and more muscular than it looks. Long, slim paws and hind legs which are slightly longer than the front ones. Oval shaped feet. The tail, which is only 4-5 centimetres (1.5 to 2 inches) long, doubles in length and volume when unfurled.

## Head

Triangular shaped with straight ears and a rounded muzzle. The nose is long and the cheekbones prominent. The eyes, which are extremely bright, are oval shaped and usually green or yellowy green.

## Coat

Medium length coat, dense and soft. Slight undercoat. Colour is very important to the Japanese. The Mike (meaning three) coat - tricoloured ginger, white and black - is considered to be a sign of good luck.

# BRITISH SHORTHAIR

This is the original ordinary British domestic cat. No longer a moggy since it became accepted as a breed in 1929. The date of its appearance in the British Isles is unknown and, although allowed in cat shows, it was definitely the poor relation until, at a congress of the Governing Council of the Cat Fancy, a member persuaded the G.C.C.F. to recognise the breed. In Europe the equivalent cat had to wait much longer; in France, for instance, it was not recognised until 1983.

The British Shorthair is a solid sort of cat with a confident look, ready for anything. It has proved its intelligence by the way in which it survives the dangers of the street when left to itself. It has often had to solve unexpected problems instantly and can obviously think on its feet! Living in a family it always knows just how far it can go and how much it can get away with. It shows great affection to its owners and also to children

(with whom it will play) and other members of the family, even the family dog. But it never loses its dignity and soon lets you know if you go too far!

It has no special care or feeding requirements other than the general rule of weighed quantities of food served at regular times every day.

### General

Solidly and powerfully built. Short, sturdy paws. Well proportioned, thick tail.

### Head

Round and solid. Strong neck. Ears set wide apart. Calm eyes.

### Coat

Short, thick hair. May be any colour.
There are innumerable. varieties of the breed.

# BOMBAY • BURMILLA

The **Bombay** looks like a black panther that never grew up. Everything about it is black: body, head, paws and nose. Everything, that is, except its fascinating golden eyes.

The only Indian thing about it though is its name. It first saw the light of day in the home of a well known American cat breeder, Mrs Nikki Horner, who crossed sable Burmese with American Shorthairs. It first began to be recognised as a breed in 1976.

Although it has the physical attributes of a black panther the Bombay is, in fact, as well behaved as it is beautiful. Easy to look after, it is affectionate, intelligent and very close to its owner. A little too much so sometimes. It can be a character!

Its fine, silky coat should be brushed every second day. A wool rag or soft glove, slightly damped, may be used to give a shine to its coat.

The Bombay gets on with other family pets – as long as they are not cats!

The **Burmilla** is a breed which is not presently recognised but soon will be. It is English and is the result of an accidental mating between a lilac Burmese and a Chinchilla, in 1981. Four kittens were born with short hair which, as they grew to maturity, turned to a wonderful silver colour: the start of a new breed of cat.

8  A gentle, affectionate, calm animal, the Burmilla fits happily into the family. From the Chinchilla it gets it habit of "chatting" to its owner. A fun cat, it loves to play with children but is nervous of strangers. It needs company and should never be left alone for any length of time. Brushing twice a week and a weighed diet will keep it healthy. It likes lots of space without being a wanderer.

13  ## BOMBAY

### General

Medium sized, muscular and well proportioned body. Straight, medium length tail. The male is larger than the female.

### Head

Round and wide with a short muzzle. Ears set well apart. Round, wide apart eyes, their colour being shades of yellow to amber.

### Coat

Fine, short, satiny hair which is black all over with no mark, stripe or spot of any other colour. Black nose and paws.
**Photos: 1, 3, 4, 6, 8, 10, 12 & 13**

## BURMILLA

### General

Medium sized with a straight back. Fairly heavy bone structure. Medium sized feet with oval paws. Medium long tail with a rounded end.

### Head

Slightly rounded with a square muzzle. Big, wide based ears which are rounded. Eyes may be any shade of green.

### Coat

Silver or golden with pronounced markings. Soft textured. Basic colours of the Burmese.  **Photos: 2, 7, 9, 11 & 14**

# BURMESE

**W**hen it first appeared in a Paris cat show in 1957, it was called a Sable cat, since the fine texture and colouring of its fur was reminiscent of the Siberian sable. Today the description no longer fits the Burmese as breeders have succeeded in rearing it in many other colours. It is none the less an extremely fine cat.

Its origins go back into history but the breed in its present form was introduced in 1930. Dr Thompson, an American, brought back a half Siamese, half Malayan female cat from Rangoon called Wong-Mau. In San Francisco he mated her several times, and by crossing mother and son managed to obtain a litter of dark brown kittens with not a spot of any other colour on them. Christened Burmese, the breed soon developed in the United States, but the Second World War interrupted its development in Europe. It made its European début in London in 1947.

The Burmese is nicknamed the "silken cat" for its fine and soft fur. But it possesses many other qualities, too. Intelligent, very aware of what is going on around it, it has proved its friendliness towards other family pets. It gets on well with dogs and will even play with them. It loves its own family but keeps its distance with strangers until it has a chance to sum them up. It appears to enjoy

travelling by car or train. Given the opportunity it will go off on its own but never very far. In fact it adapts to any lifestyle.

Its beautiful coat needs looking after. It should be thoroughly, but not too vigorously, brushed every second day and have a woollen rag run over it to give a gloss. The cat needs careful checking over once a week. Burmese do best on carefully weighed quantities of food, served at the same time every day. While still growing they should also receive vitamins.

## General

Of svelte but solid build. Slim legs, longer at the back than the front. Fairly long tail with no kink in the end.

## Head

Triangular with a jutting forehead. Ears set well apart. The large, shining eyes may be any shade of yellow but no other colour.

## Coat

Very short, fine hair. Glossy and soft to the touch. Colours now include blue, cream, chocolate, ginger, lilac etc.

# CALIFORNIA SPANGLED CAT

The California Spangled Cat was specially bred for those who dream of keeping a leopard at home – even though they know it is impossible. A Hollywood scriptwriter on a trip to Africa was horrified to find that the last black leopards were in danger of extinction. He had the idea of reproducing them, but in miniature. Attempts at crossing Siamese Sealpoints, British Shorthairs and American Shorthairs, resulted in a spotted cat which looked more or less like a leopard. It was given the name of California Spangled Cat. The addition of Egyptian blood, and that of a small African feline, was to give it an even stronger look of the leopard.

The breeder, Paul Casey, was not just after the glory of producing a new breed. He sold his cats through a big chain store with the advertising slogan "the leopard in your living room". While some protests were made about this, it was extremely successful and Paul Casey was to see his cat accepted by the International Cat Association.

The California Spangled Cat has, therefore, at least in part of the world, become a recognised breed. It is by no means lacking in good qualities either. Firstly, it is an extremely beautiful animal and can move with surprising speed. Its coat, which can be any of eight colours, is spotted in a pattern of regular lines which may differ from one animal to another. Its head is particularly fine, with eyes that are full of expression.

This short haired cat poses no particular problems of care. A weekly brush keeps it sleek. It needs a carefully weighed meat diet served at regular times every day.

The California Spangled Cat needs plenty of exercise. It may be kept in an apartment but is happiest with a garden and trees, as it loves to climb up onto a branch and observe the world.

As the breed is not developed or recognised in many places, standards are still undetermined. The body, however, is very strong and more muscular than it at first appears. The feet are long, the hind ones being longer than the front. The head is fine, triangular in shape with big, wide eyes, well opened ears, long whiskers and a dark pink nose. The markings are normally in bands but may also be rectangular or triangular. The coat, soft to the touch, is short, except on the belly and the tail where it is almost medium long haired. Colours may include silver, black, slate grey, golden, ginger, blue and brown.

# CHARTREUSE

The Chartreuse cat is French by origin, although it bears a strong resemblance to other breeds such as the British Blue and is sometimes confused with them.

It is in fact a Parisian cat, since it was bred by nuns of the Chartreuse order, whose convent was once situated on the present site of the Gardens of Luxembourg. Once classed as an ordinary European domestic cat it is now a sought-after archetypal breed.

The Chartreuse has a good head with full cheeks which give it a rounded appearance. The French writer Colette, who loved the Chartreuse, described it as "my little teddy bear with its cheeks full". Neither restless nor noisy, it gives a surprising impression of quiet strength when it moves. The Chartreuse sounds a tranquil note in its home, the symbol of quiet repose. It loves to take a nap on a cushion by its owner's side – to whom it is obviously devoted. It will go for walks with its owner, just like a dog, and has been called a "dog in a cat suit"!

It is inclined to be a wanderer but never vanishes for long. Away from its beloved owner it can, like the Siamese, literally waste away. It will, however, recover

of its own accord once home again and is soon playing and hunting as before.

To keep the woolly look to its coat, it should be brushed twice a week and should also be carefully checked over, since the thickness of the coat can encourage and hide parasites.

Rarely ill, the Chartreuse has a good appetite. Its meals need to be weighed and planned if it is not to become obese. It needs meals which are low in raw meat and include raw and cooked vegetables. Avoid fatty or starchy foods and pork.

## General

Strong and solidly built with a thick neck. Medium sized, muscular paws. The male, much heavier and stronger than the female, can weigh as much as 6 kilos (13 pounds). Medium long tail, slightly rounded.

## Head

Not as round as it looks. Ears placed high on the head but sloping. Solid jaw and almost black mouth. The wide-open, round, bright eyes are orange or amber. Blue grey nose.

## Coat

Short haired, glossy and like velvet to the touch, it is unique to the breed. The undercoat, which is the same colour, is very thick. Colours go from grey to blue grey, the most sought after being light bluish grey. There should be no shading, marking or tipping.

The blue cream Chartreuse is very popular.

# BENGAL CAT

The original Bengal was a feral cat – impossible to tame one would have said – all teeth and claws and ready to attack anyone or anything foolish enough to approach – human or animal.

Today the cat known as the Bengal is tame if not entirely peaceful, but it is not of course the same cat. There are strong points of resemblance but it is the result of multiple cross breedings. Even Mrs Jean Mill, who produced the first cat with the characteristics of the little Asian wildcat, only did so after many crosses. However, she maintains that the basis of her breed was a genuine Bengal cat. It is difficult to believe that, even captured very young, it would not have been as wild when adult.

The Bengal does look like its wild brother, however. It has clearly drawn markings, sometimes random, sometimes fanning out from a central point. Large and solid, it has muscular paws. The head is triangular with a firm chin and wide apart rounded ears, which incline slightly outward. The almost almond shaped eyes are usually yellow or amber. The tail is long and ringed.

This cat now – after two or three generations – has acquired a more-or-less calm temperament and breeders are sure that it will become an affectionate little animal ready to live quite happily with its owners.

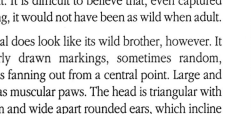

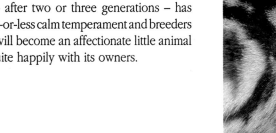

There is no final standard established as yet for the Bengal. Large and muscular, with a triangular head with rounded contours, it is distinguished mainly by its coat, where darker markings contrast with a lighter background colour. They may be brown or black, reddish brown or dark yellow, even orange. The eyes, lips and nose are outlined in black.

We are told that the Bengal will soon make an acceptable pet and that the price - rather high at the moment - will come down enough to make it affordable.

# MANX CAT

**M**any tales have been told to explain the absence of the Manx Cat's tail. One tradition is that this cat from the Isle of Man was late for the Ark and had its tail chopped off as Noah closed the hatch; another that soldiers on the island used the cats' tails as cockades, and so a mother cat took her kittens up into the mountains and chewed off their tails herself; another that the Manx Cat, which moves with a hopping gait, is in fact half rabbit ....

The more likely explanation is that it is due, as with the ears of the Scottish Fold, to genetic factors, though which gene is responsible has not been determined.

But why should they be found on the Isle of Man? Another legend claims that they are the descendants of Spanish ships' tailless cats which survived the defeat of the Spanish Armada, swimming ashore to the Island, where they multiplied.

In fact, many early histories mention tailless cats in different parts of the world: China, Siam, Japan and even Europe. And strangely, two completely tailless cats can give birth to kittens with short or even normal tails. Which is why there are two classes of Manx Cat: those which are tailless and those which have a stump of a tail.

There are very few Manx Cats left on the island, as many were transported to England by breeders eager to produce new varieties. The Manx cat looks like a tabby moggy, particularly when sitting down! When it moves it jumps or leaps up, depending on whether it is going to walk or run. This is because the back legs are longer than the front.

Domesticated, the Manx has become a charming pet. Intelligent, affectionate, home loving, it is happy even shut in an apartment. But it has kept the hunting instinct, relic of its many years of independence.

The fur of the Manx is very soft to the touch. It should be gently brushed two or three times a week.

## General

Solid, compact and muscular with a rounded back end.

## Head

Wide and round head. Long nose, solid neck. Round, bright eyes.

## Coat

Compact with a good texture and the hair is fine. May be any colour.

In Europe the Manx is classed as rumpy (tailless) or stumpy (with a stump of a tail). In America there is also the riser (with a few caudal vertebrae), the longy (short tailed) and even the tailed.

# EGYPTIAN MAU

In 1957 Princess Nathalie Troubetski disembarked in New York with two cats called Ludol and Gepa, said to be direct descendants of those sacred cats of ancient Egypt whose effigy or statuette was kept by every family as a house god. The cats were received with acclaim in America, but in fact the origins of the breed prove to be rather more recent.

Ludol and Gepa had one peculiarity: they carried on their foreheads the sacred mark of the scarab. This beetle pattern is in fact a tabby marking not unusual in some cats, and is probably a causal factor in the choice of the cat as an object of worship. They founded a line and the Egyptian Mau breed became officially recognised in the United States in 1968.

The Egyptian Mau's profile resembles that of the Abyssinian, and beneath its elegant outer appearance is a very muscular body. Adult cats make charming companions: calm, affectionate and sociable. Their voice is melodious and only used to good purpose, as for instance when they want to attract their owner's attention. Slightly reserved with strangers, they do know how to play the fool sometimes and make the family take notice!

Extremely clean, the Mau spends a lot of time at its toilet. An occasional brush, in the direction of the hair, is all the grooming it needs. The diet needs to varied and the quantity of food weighed out. Like most cats the Mau is a good hunter.

It is still, unfortunately, little known in Europe.

## General
In build very like the Abyssinian, svelte and elegant. The paws are long.

## Head
A rounded triangle in shape with a small chin. The whiskers are very long and a notable feature. The scarab pattern on the forehead is not clearly defined. The eyes are slightly almond shaped and very brilliant. Normally green eyed, yellow and hazel are also acceptable.

## Coat
The texture is fine, dense, silky and glossy. The pattern is spotted with one or two rings. It may be any of three colours: silver, with charcoal markings and green eyes; smoke, with black markings and green eyes, or bronze, with chocolate or dark brown markings and green eyes.

# EUROPEAN

Since it became a recognised breed, this one time alley cat has not really changed its ways. Perhaps it does not haunt the streets and roof tops as much as it used to – it knows that it can find guaranteed bed and breakfast and shelter in many houses! At cat shows it is no longer the poor relation, even if it does get lost sometimes among the thousands of breeds now recognised.

No longer Rudyard Kipling's "the cat who walks alone", it is fast losing the unjustified reputation of being sly, hypocritical, cruel and the familiar of witches and demons.

Brought into the home, it has shown some hitherto unsuspected qualities. Capable of being the most faithful friend to its owner, it is always an agreeable companion, taking care to maintain its own place in the family without abusing it. The cat does, nevertheless, occasionally remind one that it is still a free spirit by taking off on its own, sometimes for days on end. Perhaps in order to sharpen those wits which over the centuries have helped it win the battle for survival. There are numerous cases of cats wandering off, sometimes for long periods, and then suddenly reappearing and taking up their daily routine again as if nothing had happened. For this reason, the European domestic cat should always be free to roam if it wishes, even when it is happily settled to family life.

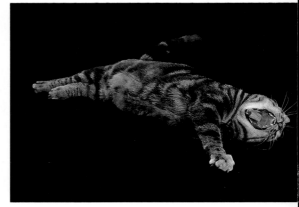

They are naturally clean animals, but it is still a good idea to give them a brush over or a comb out (in the case of longhairs) every two or three days and check them for wounds and parasites, particularly since they are likely to get into fights when out and about and pick up guests such as fleas.

They should be accustomed when young to a varied diet and should always have a bowl of clean water available.

## General
Well built without being heavy. Short, strong paws and a tail that is in proportion to the body.

## Head
Round and wide between the ears with a firm chin. The eyes are round, set well apart and may be any colour.

## Coat
Dense and soft to the touch. Numerous colours and mixtures of colours are acceptable. At one time an attempt was made to classify the European in seven categories, but varieties increased and everything suggests they will continue to do so.

# EXOTIC SHORTHAIR

**P**ersians and American Shorthairs mix well together and the result is the Exotic Shorthair. They were first introduced in the United States in the 1960s and recognised as a breed some years later. The Exotic Shorthair spread to Europe in the 1980s.

Not surprisingly, the Exotic Shorthair looks like a Persian but with medium to short hair. From one side of its ancestry it gets its nonchalance, from the other its taste for hunting rodents, and from both its gentle, affectionate, sociable character. It has qualities peculiar to the breed, too, liking to spend periods in quiet contemplation, and not much enjoying being played with. It has an independence of spirit which might have led to its becoming a wanderer had it not chosen to live a home life, even if that means being an apartment cat.

When it moves, the Exotic Shorthair can show a surprising turn of speed, even though it normally walks slowly as befits a part Persian. It can suddenly liven up – the American side showing!

The Exotic Shorthair, while being fond of its owner, is above all a family cat. It feels safe in the confines of the home and, since it regards friends of its family as being its friends, too, it will permit strangers to stroke it, while remaining rather reserved.

The medium long coat is easy to brush and comb out. The diet should be varied and carefully weighed to prevent overeating, as it has a tendency to obesity.

## General

Solid and stocky but elegant. Sturdy legs and a straight tail in proportion to the length of the body. Muscular shoulders and back and large, round feet.

## Head

Round, massive and well balanced. Wide skull. Very short nose. Small, wide apart eyes, slightly inclined outward. Eye colours should be in harmony with the coat and blue or amber are the most sought after.

## Coat

The medium long hair is evenly cropped, fine textured and glossy. May be any of the colours permitted for Persians, except golden or the colour of the Pekingese-faced red.

# NON-PEDIGREE CATS

Just as everyone loves a mongrel dog, so do we all take the common or garden moggy or alley cat to our hearts. Even if we are admirers of Persians or Siamese, or some other special breed, we always keep a soft spot for the cat of mixed parentage. It brings an extra something to the feline race, as many breeders know who, alongside their special interest, keep a common tabby who knows nothing about pedigrees and could not care less whether its father was a champion!

Where in fact does this cat with no family tree come from? For a long time it was thought to be a descendant of the European wildcat, because of similarities in appearance. Today we are aware of so many differences though, that even if it has a few drops of *Felis Silvestris* blood in its veins they must have been well diluted.

It is more generally believed that the common cat is descended from the Kaffrarian cat *(Felis lybica)*. This African animal may have been introduced into Europe by the Roman legions after a tour of duty in Egypt.

One could say that the common cat really belongs to a pure breed and operates a self-selection breeding programme. You only have to look at the number of perfect tabbies still around after thousands of years of breeding to see how true this is.

Often obliged to cope with unexpected difficulties, or to get itself out of danger, it has developed an ever-watchful intelligence. Left to itself it can always find food, and even when it adopts a family to live with it remains an independent animal.

The non-pedigree cat standards are wide. In fact they are similar to those for the European cat which developed from it. All that is really asked of it is that it should be well built without weakness or deformity, continue to be a good mouser and give its owners the love, friendship and fidelity of which it is capable.

It is naturally clean and has no special diet requirements.

# KORAT • SINGAPORE CAT

The **Korat** is one of the purest breeds in existence, due to the fact that for centuries it never left the province of Korat, an inaccessible, remote area of Thailand. It first left home in 1959, when two Americans succeeded in buying a few examples. No attempt has been made to change the breed in any way and it remains today exactly the same as the cat seen in early engravings.

Affectionate, happy, aware of everything going on around it, the Korat is a home-loving cat never tempted to wander far from its house or owners. Its main claim to beauty lies in the colour and texture of its coat. It needs to be given a brush twice a week and a massage daily. It needs a varied diet with a lot of meat. It is a good idea to have it vaccinated against respiratory diseases and it needs to avoid sudden fierce changes of temperature.

The **Singapore Cat** is of unhappy origin. It was once the sewer cat of Singapore. Searching for food among the rubbish, it disposed of small, disease-carrying rodents and did the job of a rubbish collector.

After the war, Americans passing through the great metropolis of South East Asia noticed the sewer cat and took it to America, where it was found to be an intelligent, handsome and faithful creature – and extremely clean. Successful attempts were then made to breed it. A cat of real character, although small it is muscular and reminiscent of the Abyssinian in appearance, having the same brown ticked coat. A tranquil, sociable, considerate animal, it adapts easily to home life in an apartment. Not difficult to feed it will eat anything it is given and should receive carefully weighed meals. The coat should be brushed and rubbed over to give it a gloss once a week.

7

14

15

8

9

## 11 KORAT

### General

Muscular and elegant without being heavy. Medium sized paws and tail.

### Head

Heart shaped with wide, round ears. Short nose. Shining green or greenish amber eyes.

### Coat

Thick and dense with no undercoat. Silky, glossy, silvery blue colour with lights in it.

**Photos: 2, 3, 5, 9, 14 & 15**

12

## SINGAPORE

### General

Small but well proportioned. Muscular legs. Medium sized straight tail.

### Head

Round with well set on ears and a firm chin. Large, slightly crossed eyes.

### Coat

Short haired, silky, dense and single colour with brown ticking. Most usual colour: ivory with brown ticking.

**Photos: 1, 4, 6, 7, 8, 10, 11, 12, 13 & 16**

10

13

16

# OCICAT

Geneticists, particularly amateurs, love to mix different breeds! From an American came the idea of crossing a female Abyssinian with some Siamese blood in her with a male which had several doses of Siamese in its parentage – notably chocolate Siamese – plus some Ocelot. From this hotch-potch was born a kitten which, since it vaguely resembled an ocelot, was christened the Ocicat. But we must not denigrate the Ocicat, which is in its own right a beautiful cat. With its attractive markings and the piercing expression of its eyes, it seems to have retained the best qualities of each of its ancestors. Even if one does not agree with the

random crossing of several breeds in this way, it must be admitted that this particular result is not to be disdained. The Ocicat, an impressive animal weighing 5-7 kilos (12-15 pounds) reminds one, strangely, more of the Egyptian Mau than of the Ocelot. It hides a natural vivacity under a placid appearance. Very sociable and attached to its adopted family, it becomes withdrawn once a stranger enters its orbit. While it complains if ignored, it will also grumble if pestered with too much attention. It hates disturbance and noise.

Inheriting a love of open spaces from its wilder ancestor, the Ocicat needs room to run and leap about. If it must be kept in an apartment with no garden then it should be a large, airy one.

A sturdy cat, it needs no particular care and grooming may consist of brushing twice a week. A well balanced meat diet suits it. It should be accustomed young to fresh vegetables and rice, and from to time should have fish instead of meat.

## General

Muscular and solid without being massive. Long, well proportioned feet. Long, tapering tail.

## Head

Triangular and open with a narrow muzzle. Long, pointed ears. The extremely bright eyes are golden yellow.

## Coat

Glossy and dense, the coat has dark markings on a cream background.

# ORIENTAL • HAVANA

An ancient breed, it is still not known whether the **Oriental** is the ancestor of the Siamese or a descendant of it. The breed was recognised under this name in 1970 but had been known in England for some ten years prior to this, under the general term of Foreign Shorthair (which related to any breed of Siamese type other then the Siamese itself). Lively, with very fast reactions, it is affectionate but is a one person cat, and if away from its owner for long can become nervous and even aggressive. But it is an attractive animal with a strong personality. Litters tend to be numerous, sometimes a female will give birth to six precocious kittens.

The Oriental has its followers, notably in the United States, where there are no less than twenty-six different colours classified.

It only needs an occasional brush. A sturdy cat, it does best on well-balanced, varied meals which alternate fish and meat as the main ingredient.

The **Havana,** too, is a variety of Oriental with, somewhere along the line, an injection of common or garden blood. It lived at one time in South East Asia and was bred as early as 1814 in England, under the name of the Chestnut Brown.

It is sometimes confused with the Burmese, but in fact several differences exist between the two: the shape of the head, colour of the eyes and the texture and colour of the coat, etc.

Poets sang of the ancient Havana as a creature that brought good luck. It re-emerged in Europe around 1950. A lively, playful animal, devoted to its owner, it has a wailing call and the female chatters to her kittens. It dislikes noise or shouting. There are no dietary problems and a brush once a week suffices. It will be all the happier if it has access to the outdoors.

## 10 ORIENTAL

As there is such a wide variety of Orientals, there is no strictly defined standard for the breed. The body looks extremely supple and slim. The paws are not very flat and the back legs are slightly longer than the front. The tail is long and thin. The head is roughly triangular in shape with a well defined profile and almond shaped green eyes. The coat, flat and glossy, has well distributed markings. On the tabby Oriental the sacred scarab mark of the Egyptian Mau can be seen.

**Photos: 2, 3, 4, 5, 6, 7, 8, 9, 10 & 12**

## HAVANA
### General

Slim but muscular. Medium long legs and tail. Compact, oval feet.

### Head

Long, well proportioned, with a muzzle that is longer than it is wide. Ears set quite well apart. Brilliant green eyes.

### Coat

Smooth, glossy self colour coat. Colours go from a dark chestnut brown to rich reddish chestnut.

**Photos: 1, 11 & 13**

# CORNISH REX • DEVON REX SELKIRK REX

Geneticists in Germany, France and England have all produced curly coated cats over the years, going back to just before the Second World War. Undoubtedly the most successful of these are the Cornish Rex and the Devon Rex.

The first Cornish Rex recorded was born in Cornwall in 1950, and its curly coat was in fact a spontaneous genetic mutation. It was to found a long and wide line of Rex cats (so called because of the likeness of the curly coat to that of the curly coated Astrex rabbit) which spread throughout Europe and the United States. Ten years later in Devon, a different variety of Rex was to be bred from the descendants of a curly coated tom living wild in a tin mine and a domestic female. The female, a tortoiseshell and white, gave birth to a litter of kittens, one of which was curly coated. It was to join a Rex breeding programme and become the founder of the Devon Rex line.

The main difference between these two breeds is that the Devon Rex has a wide face and little, short nose, while the Cornish Rex has a long, Roman nose. In both cases the curly coat is in fact the soft undercoat; true Rexes have no top coat or guard hair.

In the United States a number of breeders have worked on producing an American Rex. In 1987 they finally succeeded and, although as yet unrecognised, the Selkirk Rex has been a great success with the public at American cat shows. In temperament it is a fun-loving, even naughty cat, which can be calm and affectionate when the occasion demands.

### CORNISH REX
#### General
Solid, hard, long, supple body. Long, straight legs with small, oval feet. Long, thin tail.

#### Head
Longer than it is wide. Flat topped skull and hollow cheeks. Strong chin with long, curling whiskers. Big ears, set high. Gleaming, oval eyes.

#### Coat
Short and dense. May be curly, frizzy or wavy. Symmetrical markings. May be any colour.
**Photos: 5, 9, 10, 11, 13 & 14**

### DEVON REX
#### General
Firm, muscular body. Long, thin paws. Back legs slightly longer than front. Small, oval feet.

#### Head
Prominent cheekbones, short muzzle, firm chin and full cheeks. Big ears and curly whiskers and eyebrows. Shining, oval eyes.

#### Coat
Wavy and soft to the touch with no guard hairs. May be any colour.
**Photos: 1, 2, 6, 7 & 12**

### SELKIRK REX
Strict standards for the Selkirk Rex have not yet been established. It is medium sized with a strong bone structure and heavy jaws. The kittens are born curly coated. The muscular body is covered with a thick, curly coat reminiscent of a sheep. May be any colour. A large Selkirk Rex may weigh 5-8 kilos (11-18 pounds).
**Photos: 3, 4, 8 & 15**

# SCOTTISH FOLD

**B**ack in the last century a sailor brought back a cat from China, from the Province of Pet Chi Li, with folded down ears. Enquiries made in that country revealed that the Chinese cat was of no particular breed. Moreover, it was a unique example of which no trace remained. This, up until 1961, was the only known example of a cat with ears that folded down against its head. In that year a Scottish shepherd, William Ross, noticed in a litter of kittens one female which had curious, folded over ears. He kept her, christened her Susie, and when she was adult mated her. Disappointed at first with her two kittens, which seemed to be born with normal ears, he discovered that at four weeks old the ears folded down of their own accord. The Scottish Fold breed was born. Geneticists have since scientifically shown that this anomaly is due to a gene which is transmittable to European cats.

Today the Scottish Fold, although it is not recognised everywhere, has a number of followers and enthusiastic breeders, and many people admire it, pointing out that the folded down ears give the cat an additional charm all of its own.

The Scottish fold is a family cat. It loves the people around it, and like many cats is particularly devoted to its owner. Tranquil, sociable, even with other family pets, it is a home-loving cat. The folded ears give it a slightly sad look at variance with its happy nature. It makes a formidable mouser.

Sturdy and easy to feed, it is resistant even to fierce changes of temperature. A weekly brush is enough to keep its fur clear.

## General

Short and plump in form. Medium long legs and round feet. Medium long tail in proportion with the body.

## Head

Large and round with a medium nose and firm chin. The ears must be well folded down, forwards (in rare cases the ear hangs down). Round, wide eyes, set well apart, with a particularly sweet expression. The eye colour should be in harmony with that of the coat.

## Coat

Very soft to the touch, dense and may be any colour.

# SPHYNX

**I**t has been said that the Sphynx is a pretty name for an ugly cat! You either like the Sphynx or you don't. Contrary to belief, it is not a recent phenomenon: hairless cats have been known for centuries, and usually one found in a litter would be got rid of quickly, except by the Aztecs, who venerated and protected hairless cats.

In 1935 a French breeder introduced a breed of hairless cat, and in 1966 a successful line was produced by a Canadian breeder, which was known as the Canadian Hairless or Sphynx. Sought after by their admirers, they fetch very good prices.

Their lack of fur, happily, has had no ill effects on the character or qualities of this affectionate, sociable and gentle animal. The Sphynx loves people who love it. A timid cat, it is inclined to avoid strangers.

It needs to be kept indoors, since its lack of hair makes it vulnerable to the cold and to draughts. It should live in conditions where temperature changes are slight. It does not get on well with other family pets, such as dogs or other cats, and it is unfair to keep a Sphynx with other animals as it is likely to become even more nervous.

In other respects the Sphynx's care poses no real problems. It needs a daily wipe over with a damp cloth and its eyes should be regularly checked. Its meals should be carefully weighed, alternating between fresh food and tinned, and should always include fresh vegetables. It should not be overfed.

As it is a rare breed, the hairless cat does not have any strict standard except for the coat, and even there there is some licence allowed.

## General

Slim bodied and standing tall. The musculature is light and fine and the neck is particularly loose. Long, well-set-on tail.

## Head

Triangular and dominated by big ears. Whiskers are either absent or very small and fine. Wide open eyes, usually green, hazel or golden.

## Coat

No hair on the body, but very short, plush hair may appear on the face, ears, tail and along the spine. May be any colour. Markings are directly on the skin, which feels nice to the touch and may be slightly wrinkled.

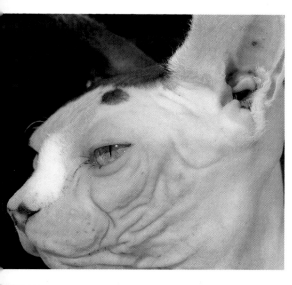

# TONKINESE

**O**nce very well known but fallen out of favour for a while, the Tonkinese is again appearing at cat shows. In Switzerland in particular, breeders are once more developing this Siamese/Burmese cross. It has the markings of the former which fade into the coat of the latter.

Physically the Tonkinese looks more like the Siamese than the Burmese. The markings are very clear even though they may shade into the colour of the coat, for which reason the cat's colour is sometimes referred to as monochrome.

A lively and affectionate cat. It gets its friendly nature from the Burmese rather than its more standoffish cousin the Siamese. It is interested in everything that goes on around it. The Tonkinese loves company and lots of space to run around.

It needs an occasional brush over and should be fed a balanced diet which alternates fresh and tinned food.

There are five different colours of Tonkinese.

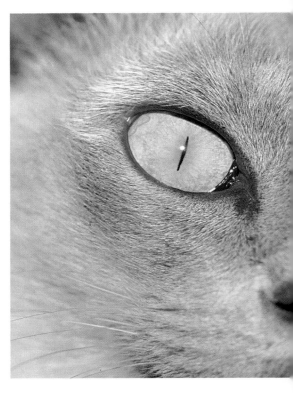

## General

Medium long, muscular body. The male, which is bigger than the female, has a very muscular neck and shoulders. Back legs slightly longer than front. Long, tapering tail.

## Head

Triangular shape with ears set wide apart, square muzzle and almond shaped, aquamarine eyes.

## Coat

Soft, shining and thick, gradually paling to a lighter shade on the underside of the body. Colour combinations as follows:- natural mink: rich brown, lightenining on the underbelly, with dark chocolate to sable markings and dark brown undersides to the feet; champagne mink: cream beige to chamois, with brown markings, pinkish to light brown undersides to feet; blue mink: soft bluey grey to blue shades, markings of a darker shade to the body, from mid to slate blue, underside of feet blue grey; honey mink: golden to amber shades, apricot being preferred, medium to dark reddish brown markings, underside of feet flesh coloured; platinum mink: pale silvery grey, slight beige overtone permitted, loosely defined markings, underside of feet flesh coloured with rosy pink overtone permitted.

# MEDIUM LONGHAIRS

# BALINESE

The origin of some breed names can be surprising, as is the case with the Balinese, which has never, even in the remotest past, had the slightest connection with the Indonesian island of Bali!

In 1930 an argument sprang up between certain American breeders of pure bred Siamese and others who claimed to be producing a longhair variety. The former won their case on the basis that to call the second longhair Siamese would lead to confusion and, forced to capitulate, the latter followed the suggestion of one of their members for a new name. He suggested that as the cat had "the grace of a Balinese dancer" the breed should be named the Balinese. He had obviously never seen the delightful Balinese dancers with their mechanical gestures!

And was this longhaired Siamese the result of an accident or deliberate cross breeding? The question has never been answered but the result is delightful. The Balinese is a very beautiful creature with clear markings, a fine head and a thick coat.

As intelligent as the Siamese, friendly, naturally happy and active, when playing it can produce some incredibly acrobatic jumps. Its tendency to need exercise of this kind to keep it relaxed means it needs plenty of space. If living in an apartment it should have at least a terrace, courtyard or preferably garden to play in. The Balinese is not by nature a wanderer, it is too attached to its adopted family.

The Balinese's coat rarely gets tangled but it should be brushed daily and, of course, checked over carefully once a week. Like all cats related to the Siamese, it loves fish which should be fed alternately with meat meals.

## General

Medium size, longish body which is muscular but still elegant. Long, fluffy tail.

## Head

Triangular with wide based ears and a small but well defined chin. Almond shaped eyes are the magnificent blue of the Siamese.

## Coat

Fluffy and thick but with no undercoat. Colours as for the Siamese: sealpoint, blue point, lilac point and chocolate point. Other colour variations of the Balinese are called Javanese – because Java is not far from Bali!

# MAINE COON

The sturdy Maine Coon cat has been established for more than a century and is one of the oldest American breeds. It is extremely popular in its home country. From a distance it looks a little like a raccoon, which is where it gets its name from. This does not mean, however, that there is any raccoon blood in its veins. One tradition has it that the cat is a descendant of Marie Antoinette's pet cats, sent to America to await her possible exile there. It is more likely, however, that the first Maine Coons were ships' cats from trading ships plying between the Old World and the New. Somehow or other they must have slipped ashore unnoticed and, faced with a more severe climate than they were used to, their fur gradually grew thicker as a protection against the harsh weather.

The Maine Coon was not at first taken into American homes. It had to fend for itself, usually living wild close to a farm. Gradually they moved closer to these homesteads and their occupants until one day they found themselves accepted and adopted by the farmers.

Although the colours of the Maine Coon were not, in early days at least, the same, it has a look of the Norwegian Skogkatt and resembles it in behaviour. Mischievous, always watchful, it still has the look of a nice cat. Calm and sweet natured with its owners, it is an athletic creature, loving to climb trees in the garden or, if kept in an apartment, leaping onto the top of a cupboard. It has strong hunting instincts and loves fish so much it has been nicknamed the "fisherman's cat". Naturally it should be fed fish, alternating it with meat meals and added vegetables.

It may be brushed and combed out once a week. Its many years spent living outdoors have made it a very healthy breed.

## General

Strongly built but elegant. Short, strong paws which are often white. The large, round feet have tufts of hair between the claws. Very fluffy, plumed tail.

## Head

Round with high cheeks. Strong, well defined chin. Large, wide open, oval eyes which may be any colour, yellow being preferred.

## Coat

Dense and shorter across the shoulders than elsewhere. The texture of the hair fine and silky. Twenty-five colours are permitted plus eight tabby combinations.

# RAGDOLL

The story goes that a Persian Queen in kitten, knocked down by a car, gave birth to kittens which were, as a result of the accident, incapable of feeling pain or fear ever after. This North American breed certainly seems to be incapable of reacting to aggression of any sort.

It is called the Ragdoll because it can be grabbed and picked up without showing any desire to escape or scratch.

It has both Persian and Birman in its ancestry. The first Ragdolls had the long hair of the former and the white "gauntlets" of the latter, but it must be admitted that the standard for this rare breed is fairly elastic.

Sweet natured, malleable, easy to look after, perhaps a little too lethargic, the Ragdoll is the perfect apartment cat. Breeders say even that it is an absolute baby! Its medium long coat needs brushing and combing out every day. Sturdier than it looks, it only needs a varied, carefully weighed diet of alternating fish and meat meals with fresh vegetables or rice, to keep it healthy.

The Ragdoll is still not well known, perhaps because the breed is still developing, as can be seen from the standard given for it. Apart from the obvious Persian and Birman influence there is clearly some Siamese, too. This means it can be classified in the same groups as the Siamese: seal point, blue point, lilac point and chocolate point.

### General

A body that is supple to the point of being limp. Moderately plump. Strong, fluffy tail.

### Head

Rounded, with wide cheeks and a short nose. Ears set well apart. Clear blue, wide open eyes.

### Coat

Thick rather than long. Very fluffy. In addition to the Siamese colourings they may also be bicoloured and multicoloured.

# BIRMAN

T he story of the sacred Birman cat begins with a lovely legend which is also the story of how it got its name.

Long ago in Cambodia there lived a rule of monks, known as *kittahs*. They belonged to the cult of the god Song Ho, but also worshipped Tsun Kian Tse, the sapphire-eyed goddess. In their vast monastery lived a hundred sacred cats whose job it was to receive the souls of dead monks, who later would be reincarnated. Each kittah therefore had his own cat, as did a very saintly old monk, Mun Ha, who, accompanied by his white cat Sinh, passed his hours in meditation at the feet of Tsun Kian Tse.

The kittahs' reputation for holiness was well established in Cambodia and infuriated the Brahmans, whose practices did not bear such close scrutiny. One day they attacked the kittahs, killing great numbers of them. Those who were able to escaped with their cats and built an underground temple to Tsun Kian Tse in Birman. One night raiders attacked the temple and Mun-Ha was killed. As the holy man died, Sinh placed his feet upon his fallen master and faced the golden goddess. As he did so the hairs of his body turned golden and his yellow eyes became sapphire blue like hers; his four white legs turned earthy brown – but where his feet rested gently on his dead master they remained white as a symbol of purity. The next day all the cats in the temple had turned golden and Sinh did not leave his master until, seven days later, he died and carried his master's soul into paradise. From that day to this, the Birman cat has had white feet and blue eyes!

The Birman is in fact the result of crosses between Persians and Siamese, one of which at least had white feet.

But it is the sheer beauty of the cat which has guaranteed its ever-increasing popularity. Its sumptuous coat and piercing blue gaze go with an equally lovely temperament.

## General

Long, fairly large body with solid, medium length feet. Round, firm paws. The white glove marks should be well defined and clear. On the front feet the white should not go beyond the last phalanx, while on the back legs it finishes at a point just under the foot. The medium long tail is extremely fluffy.

## Head

Round, wide and solid with a domed forehead and a short nose. Small, slightly rounded ears. The eyes must be the characteristically piercing and fascinating blue of the Birman.

## Coat

Beautiful, silky textured with medium long hair, particularly luxuriant around the neck and on the fluffy tail. The back and flanks are well covered, too, and the hair is slightly wavy on the belly. The ruff should be well defined. Seal point markings on a light background colour.

Breeders are, of course, hastening to produce other colour combinations: blue point, lilac point and chocolate point. There is an American shorthair Birman, called variously Snowshoe or Silver Lace, which is not yet recognised worldwide.

# BIRMAN (cont'd)

Gentle and sociable by nature, the Birman is very attached to its family and will of its own accord go up to visitors it likes and ask to be stroked. It accepts other family pets, even other cats, but keeps a close eye on them. If its owner favours another cat it will not extend its claws but shows its unhappiness by a totally genuine display of sulks. Needless to say it adores its owner. It will play with children if not teased too much. It should never be restrained against its will.

Perfectly happy living in a flat, the Birman also likes a garden or courtyard. It rarely miaows, and when it does it does so quietly.

The Birman should really be brushed every two days to keep its coat in good condition. It should be carefully checked over once a week. It is not a greedy cat and does not show much interest at meal times. It should be fed at regular times every day and the diet should be a well balanced and carefully weighed meat diet, interspersed occasionally with fish.

When the female is in season it can come as something of a shock, as the cat's normal behaviour totally changes. Kittens are born with a very pale, single coloured coat. The Siamese-style markings only appear after a few weeks.

# NORWEGIAN SKOGKATT

Not until it ventured out from the fastnesses of its Norwegian forests did the myths surrounding the Skogkatt become dispelled and it could be seen that it was not really a wild and savage monster weighing some 20 kilos (45 pounds)!

The story of the Skogkatt goes back hundreds of years. It was the cat of the Vikings, who imported it from the shores of the Caspian Sea. Once their ships touched dry land again the cats were freed to look after themselves as best they could. They took shelter in the deepest forests, where they lived a rough but free existence. Their coat, already thick and fluffy, became much thicker to combat the cold of the long, hard Norwegian winters. The cat must also have learned to protect itself against the dangers of living in the wild. It hardly ever came out of hiding, only occasionally approaching some farm in search of food. People allowed it to live in peace but made no attempt to domesticate it – nor did it want to be domesticated.

The Skoggkatt, recognised as a wild but useful animal, was given official protection. Norwegian forestry guards had orders to watch over it and make sure it was not captured and taken out of the country. However, around 1930, breeders began to be interested in it.

Some examples of the breed were smuggled out of the country, and the first European Skogkatt Club was formed by a Madame Rohiff. Other breeders succeeded in obtaining these Viking cats, too, (probably by bribing certain forestry guards). Being an extremely handsome cat it was soon a great success, not only in Europe but in the United States as well.

The breed was given recognition in 1977 by the Féderation Féline Internationale. Breeders multiplied and the cat spread without, happily, too many new varieties being produced. Seeing the great admiration and interest it always creates at cat shows, one can predict a very successful future for the cat which is "not like others" – even though, at a distance, it can be mistaken for a European cat.

In fact the Skogkatt may be described as of a type which is halfway between the wild European cat and the Lynx – partly because it has the latter's typical ears tipped with long hair, and also because it looks bigger than it is. The impression is heightened by the way it leaps and jumps and races about hunting. Even the domesticated version has an astonishing ability to climb at amazing

## General

Long, solid, supple body. Long feet which are slightly longer at the back than the front.

## Head

Triangular shape with well defined nose and a solid chin. The big, wide open eyes may be any colour.

## Coat

Long, fluffy and waterproof with a woolly undercoat. May be any colour and may have white markings on the paws, chest and belly. In summer the under coat moults, returning to its usual thickness in winter.

Females are slightly smaller than males. Kittens look very much like ordinary European cats but develop quickly to reach full maturity at two years old.

# NORWEGIAN SKOGKATT (cont'd)

speed and descend from a tree at the same rate. Its big, strong claws help it to hook itself on when jumping from branch to branch, or clinging to a rocky perch. Hunting and racing around is essential to the cat's wellbeing, which is why it should always have access to a big garden with trees. It can live in an apartment but will not be happy.

This is a very intelligent cat, much attached to its home, but one whose legacy of long years in the wild has left it nervous of strangers, to the extent that it will disappear immediately visitors appear. Young Skogkatts like to play, but only when they feel like it. The same goes for caresses, which they won't take for too long.

The Skogkatt virtually never gets a tangled coat. A brush and comb out once a week suffices to keep it well groomed except during moulting. The moult is radical, only the tail remaining really fluffy. But the new coat grows very quickly.

It likes a meat diet, occasionally interspersed with fish meals.

# SOMALI

The Somali is quite simply a longhaired Abyssinian. Some people believe they are the result of crosses between Abyssinians and Persians, others that it is due to the accidental presence in an Abyssinian of the gene that determines long hair, as has been seen occasionally in other shorthaired breeds. Normally a breeder finding a longhaired kitten in an Abyssinian litter would eliminate it as not conforming to the standard and never mention it again.

In 1930, however, an American breeder had two simultaneous litters, from different queens, each of which contained a longhaired kitten, one male and one female. As soon as possible they were mated and so were their offspring in their turn. And the day came when litters from this line produced only longhaired cats. In 1963 the Somali was given official recognition as a breed. Today it can be seen at cat shows everywhere and is deservedly successful. It has kept the Abyssinian ticking in a different form: the long hair showing it as clear colour markings, which are usually in two or three bands and do not appear immediately.

If you ask any cat lover which good qualities their cat, be it Siamese, Persian or any other breed, exhibits, the inevitable reply will be – all of them! In the case of the Somali it would be true. Firstly, it has kept all the best features of the Abyssinian. An elegant mover, it instinctively knows how to pose to the best advantage. Demanding of both its owner's affection and time it, too, can genuinely mope if its owner appears to neglect it, or is away for any length of time. It is obedient to its owner's slightest command, however quietly or unobtrusively given. It is totally unaggressive, unless really provoked, and prefers to go away rather than show the slightest bad temper.

But the Somali has its own characteristics, too. The coat is very soft to the touch and the ruff and plumed tail are

# SOMALI (cont'd)

points in favour of long hair. More affectionate and less reserved than the Abyssinian, and playful with children, it really integrates itself into the family.

An excellent hunter, it knows how to be patient and cunning.

It should be noted that the Somali is vulnerable to sudden changes of temperature and to draughts. If the cat is to be kept in an apartment, a constant, gentle room temperature should be maintained.

The Somali grooms itself, being a naturally clean cat, and only needs a quick brush over in the morning. Left to itself it would eat nothing but meat. To combat a tendency to obesity, however, it needs a balanced diet which from time to time includes fish. If it is to be kept without the benefit of a garden it should at least have the doors left open to give free access from room to room: it must have some exercise.

## General

A supple and elegant body with solid limbs and oval feet. The back is rather arched. The plumed, fluffy tail is slightly tapered at the end.

## Head

Lengthens into a narrow muzzle that is not actually pointed. Medium, wide based ears, always pricked up. The deep, almond shaped eyes, green or golden in colour, are full of expression.

## Coat

The texture is thick and fine at the same time. The bands of ticking are clearly visible. The colour is darkish brown on dark orange. The nose is brick red, outlined in black.

Although the breed is established now, it is possible that the odd shorthair will turn up in a litter one day. The coat does not reach its mature length (medium long) until the cat is eighteen months old.

# PERSIANS AND PERSIAN VARIETIES

# PERSIAN

The Persian is still the archetypal longhaired cat. It represents forty percent of all recognised cats of every breed when all its numerous varieties are included. Only common domestic breeds can rival it in numbers.

The Persian owes its popularity to its good looks, gracefulness, and elegant gait. The perfect apartment cat, it is a living ornament which enhances its surroundings and is very aware of the fact, without taking advantage of it owners. While it might be thought a lazy cat that likes to sleep a lot, closer observation reveals that it can move fast when necessary – although it prefers to amble majestically and nonchalantly through life.

While the exact origins of the Persian are unknown, it is generally thought that it is descended from the Turkish Angora cat, like that discovered in Armenia in the middle of the last century. And, by breeding from the Angora, English breeders succeeded in producing the present day cat in its three basic colours: blue, white and black. The exact dates when British breeders started to produce Persians are vague but the results have certainly been magnificent.

There are numerous colour varieties of Persian, particularly bicoloureds. The latter are now limited to six combinations, all of which have white as the base colour: black, blue, chocolate, lilac red and cream. The markings must be clearly defined and at least one third of the coat must be white. The eyes must be amber or dark orange. The nose and pads should either be pink or the same colour as the majority of the coat. Face markings on a bicolour should always include an inverted V shape. There is also a tortoiseshell and white version, known in America as a calico.

# BLACK PERSIAN • WHITE PERSIAN AND BLACK AND WHITE PERSIAN

The Black Persian is probably as old as the Blue, but has been recreated by English breeders and is thought to be the first Persian variety to have been recognised. It is certainly one of the most handsome. Unfortunately, perfect Black Persians are rarely found. From tip to tail there should not be a single white hair – the entire coat must be black as a crow. Nor must there be a mark of any other colour. The slightest brown shading in the coat is also rejected, as is a grey undercoat. The eyes must be amber or dark copper coloured.

The White Persian, also known as the French Persian, must be pure white. Originally only with blue eyes, there then appeared orange eyed white Persians followed by odd eyed ones, with one blue eye and one orange. The White Persian should not be confused with the Chinchilla with its ticked coat, which is now considered a separate breed.

White Persians have a tendency towards deafness. This is due to the dominant white gene. Its admirers affirm that it makes up for this deficiency by being extra sensitive and by a greater than usual ability to concentrate. Deafness occurs far less frequently in orange eyed Persians, which suggests that there is some link between blue eyes and the ability to hear.

Apart from differences of colour, the standard for the Black Persian and the White is identical. Whites do, however, have a tendency to be slightly longer bodied and shorter nosed.

Bicoloured Black and White Persians are easy to obtain. In Great Britain they are also found in the Pekingese-faced version, with its almost flat, wrinkly nose.

# BLUE PERSIAN AND OTHERS

**T**he Blue Persian was probably the original guinea pig used by British breeders. An eighteenth-century naturalist described it as having "a completely grey, shaded coat which is fine haired and glossy, darker on the back, with a plumy tail, the hairs of which are five or six fingers long."

Obviously they were writing about a Blue Persian with an all grey coat. The standard lays down that the coat of the Blue Persian should show all the shades of blue grey. This is the most cherished variety of Persian today, and the purity of its greyish blue – or bluish grey – coat is carefully preserved.

Today there is also a Red Persian. They are rare because it is very difficult to breed the true gingery red colour. This is a great pity because Reds, like the Persian Red Tabby, are extremely beautiful. The truly magnificent coat is true gingery red, getting darker on the head, cheeks, chest and legs. Again, with the Red Tabby breeders have great difficulty in breeding true.

# CHINCHILLA • GOLDEN SILVER

These three cats were the original Persian breeds before it became one family, and are distinguished from each other only by the colour of their coats. If you look carefully they do vary slightly in some other details, particularly the Chinchilla, but they are a close group.

The **Chinchilla** first appeared in England around 1880. The Chinchilla Cat Club was founded in 1908 and the cats began to be exported to the United States. It was not long before the breed spread to other parts of Europe, and in the numerous varieties of Chinchilla the signs of its individuality as a breed can always be seen, as well as it relationship to the Persian.

A cat of great character, it is very intelligent and will follow its owner from one room to another, chattering away to him or her. The tone of its miaows will change according to what it wants. Happy and playful, it likes lots of attention. Its very beautiful coat needs brushing every day. A healthy cat, it will fare even better given the opportunity of a garden to play in. The Chinchilla needs a balanced, carefully weighed diet.

The **Golden Shaded** Persian is the result of crossing Chinchillas and Silvers and is difficult to breed, as the kittens are likely to be born either Silver or Chinchilla. The same problem occurs when trying to breed Silvers.

It is difficult to imagine a more beautiful fur than that of the Golden Shaded Persian. The colours of the coat, underlined by a golden undercoat and darker hair ends, go beautifully together. In this cat, as in the other two, colour tipping plays a big part in the typical appearance of the coat. Colours may vary from a warm brown to apricot, softening on the mouth area and the chest.

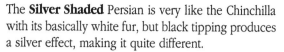

The **Silver Shaded** Persian is very like the Chinchilla with its basically white fur, but black tipping produces a silver effect, making it quite different.

The Golden and Silver Shaded Persians have the same temperament and qualities as the Chinchilla but with one difference: they make a lot less noise!

### General

Stocky body with short, thick feet and legs.

### Head

Wide, round head with a wide muzzle and short nose which is not as flat as that of the pure Persian and is brick red in colour. Big, expressive eyes, outlined in black. Usually the eyes are blue green or emerald.

### Coat

The three types differ here. The Chinchilla has an all white coat with tipping about an eighth of the way along the length. The undercoat is pure white and the whole effect is of a shining silver. The Golden Shaded has a "multicoloured" coat whose underlying shades give a wonderful effect. The Silver Shaded has "shadows" in its coat, being more ticked than the Chinchilla. There are also blue, lilac and chocolate varieties of the Silver Shaded. A further variety is the Cameo Persian, basically a Chinchilla with some red markings.

# SMOKE AND TABBY PERSIAN

New varieties of Persian keep being produced and, particularly in the United States, it seems that every breeder would like to create his own. Many of these disappear as fast as they appear, or are produced only with such difficulty that they are very rare.

This is true of the Smoke. A magnificent creature, it causes a sensation at cat shows, where it always seems to be in the medals. Usually it is the result of crossing Chinchillas and Black Persians. The undercoat is silver and the top coat black. Standing or sitting still it looks like a Black, but as soon as it moves the undercoat shows strikingly through the black, particularly in the ruff and fluffier areas. A very elegant, intelligent and sturdy cat, it is extremely affectionate towards its family. It is a lot of trouble to look after, however. The various Smoke varieties include: the blue Smoke, with blue grey coat, nose and pads; the chocolate Smoke with brown fur and nose and cinnamon coloured pads; the lilac Smoke, whose fur, nose and pads are lilac with pinkish highlights; the red Smoke, whose coat is ginger, with pink nose and pads; the cream Smoke, with cream fur and pink nose and pads; and the oyster Smoke, which also has variations. There is also a Smoke blue.

Another important group is that of the tabbies (marbled). These were first seen in a show in London in 1871. They have become more numerous since. Classic tabbies were at first silver, chestnut or ginger. Today they are classified as follows:

Persian Silver Tabby, with silver fur and clear black tipping. Lines and spiral markings appear. The shape of a letter M is outlined on the forehead and the eye is outlined in black. Varieties include blue silver tabby, chocolate silver tabby and lilac silver tabby.

Persian Brown Tabby. The colour is golden brown with black tipping, and markings resemble those of the silver tabby. There is also, of course, a blue tabby, chocolate tabby and lilac tabby.

Persian Red Tabby; very sought after in the United States but difficult to obtain. There is one variation: cream tabby.

It is impossible to list all the Persian tabby varieties, but mention should be made of the red calico, and other tortoiseshells, including the calico and dilute calico.

The Chinchillas have made their contribution to the Persian tabbies, too, with the golden, silver, shaded, shell cameo and tortoiseshell varieties.

# COLOURPOINT

For a long time – too long – the Colourpoint was the cat without a family. How should it be classified? Among the longhairs? Or was it not a Siamese which happened to have long hair? Or a Birman that lost its white gloves? It was called Colourpoint, Khmer and Himalayan, and since it was a cross breed, at the rare shows which allowed it in, it was hidden away in a corner.

But visitors remained such a long time in front of the cages of the forbidden cat, and the praises they sang of it became so difficult to ignore, that the Persian Colourpoint was finally admitted to the ranks of the great ones.

The name, which became its official title, was certainly justified, since the cat has more of the Persian in it than the Siamese. From the latter it has kept only the Siamese markings and the colour of the eyes. There is also some Birman in it, which shows in the temperament of the cat, which is very loving.

The Colourpoint is not a recent breed. A Swedish breeder was crossing Persians and Siamese as far back as 1924, and it was a long job. In 1930 two Americans started a long selection programme which eventually resulted in a longhaired cat with Siamese markings. It was christened Debutante – not without humour.

With the Second World War, which meant minds were occupied worldwide with more worrying matters than breeding new cats, the project came to a temporary halt, and it was not until 1947 that breeding attempts were continued, this time by British breeders. But the way was still not clear, and it took another eight years of work to improve the breed before the efforts of Mr Stirling Webb, in particular, were rewarded with recognition of the Persian Colourpoint by the all-powerful G.C.C.F (Governing Council of the Cat Fancy).

Many variations on the Colourpoint have appeared since then. But certain rules are observed for all of them. Physically, the cat must resemble the Persian more than the Siamese. The round head, small ears, sturdy feet and short tail are required, and Siamese markings and blue eyes are essential.

Its many admirers claim that the Colourpoint combines the calm temperament of the Persian with the vivacity of the Siamese and the affectionate nature of the Birman. In a happy family atmosphere it often becomes an important member of the household. It loves to play with children but does need long periods of rest. Friendly to all, the Colourpoint adores its owner. It will come to you with its irresistible blue gaze and gentle miaow asking to be petted; persevering gently but insistently until picked up or stroked!

The Persian Colourpoint is a solid, healthy cat, rarely ill. But the magnificent coat needs constant care. It must be brushed daily and gently but firmly combed out. Once a week it should be checked over. Its diet should consist of tinned and fresh food fed alternately. Once or twice a week it should be given fish instead of meat. Occasionally rice may replace the fresh vegetables which it also needs.

The longhair Colourpoint - also known as the Himalayan - matures at eighteen months. It has the round head of the Persian, very long whiskers and piercingly blue eyes.
The colour of markings should be as uniform as possible with the mask clearly defined.
The body is solid and set on sturdy legs. The shortish tail must have no kink in it.
The coat is luxuriant and silky and the hair about 12 centimetres (5 inches) long.
Despite its lazy look, the Colourpoint needs exercise. If no garden or yard is available it should at least be free to go from room to room. It is the ideal pet for someone living on their own.
The Persian Colourpoint can be a wonderful mouser when the occasion arises.

# COLOURPOINT VARIETIES

**K**ept, if not out of cat shows themselves, at least out of the competitions and medals for a long time, the Persian Colourpoint, nicknamed "the poor man's Birman", now figures among the greats, thanks to its handsome appearance.

Many varieties have been produced: endless permutations of the Siamese markings and also of the Persian colours. There is also a Shorthair Colourpoint with its own numerous varieties.

The longhaired varieties of this breed are also known by their old name of Himalayan and, more rarely, Kashmir. Some are variations on the well known markings of Siamese and others are more complicated. These include a tortoiseshell – or tortie point – which is what it sounds like: tortoiseshell markings on a cream body. The tabby colourpoint is known – rather flatteringly – as a Lynx point!

A general rule for all longhaired colourpoints, whose hair must be at least 12 centimetres (5 inches) long, is that the coat must be thick, luxuriant, silky and with a fluffy ruff around the neck. Markings must also be clearly defined. Kittens are always born pure white, the markings appearing at around six months.

The Shorthair Colourpoint had more complicated beginnings than its longhaired relative. To get the variation in type, crosses were made not only with Siamese but with other breeds, notably the Abyssinian. The result was a very beautiful creature with the characteristics of the Siamese but in a wider variety of coats. In addition to the usual colour combinations: seal, blue, chocolate and lilac point, were now added red point, cream point, seal lynx point, lilac lynxpoint, seal tortie point, chocolate cream point, blue cream point and lilac cream point, etc.

The standard for Shorthair Colourpoints insists that the coat be thick and at the same time fine haired and glossy.

The cat has a very elegant silhouette, a slender body, long fine paws, deep, luminous, almond shaped eyes usually ringed in white, and a long, ringed tail.

According to their owners they offer a restful change for anyone who has suffered from a demanding Siamese!

95

# ASPECTS OF THE CAT

# THE CATS OF VENICE

**T**he beautiful city of Venice has a unique army of guardian cats – despite the animal's reputation for not liking the water.

Take them away and the city of the Doges would face a new danger: that of being gnawed away by rats as well as crumbling into the sea.

Just the smell of cats is enough to frighten off the menace whose very name evokes hideous medieval images of the plague. If the cats were to disappear the rats would take over.

Of course, some people do not like the smell of cat in the ruelles between the houses either – these are the same people who, when the good weather comes, complain of the noise the tomcats make. But it is a price that has to be paid. Everyone recognises that in the fight against rodents the cat is our greatest ally.

Cats have had the best of times and the worst of times in the city of Venice. During the Inquisition, in Venice as elsewhere in Europe, the cat was not spared. The Inquisitors, who saw witchcraft everywhere, accused the mysterious creature of being in league with the Devil. Unjustly exterminated, by the time the crusaders had brought the Black Death back from the east, the cat was practically wiped out.

In the people's distress, as rats spread disease, the cats usefulness was proved. The citizens could see how essential they were to a city like Venice, where the little channels between walls and houses harboured rats and allowed them to multiply.

# THE CATS OF VENICE (cont'd)

After this a typically Venetian breed of cat developed, the result of crosses between the imported eastern cats and those native cats that still survived. Impressive, with its eyes the green of the lagoon, irresistibly reminding one of the wild cat, the Soriano – so called after the Syrian cat – has been the pride of the Venetians ever since, and they owe it an everlasting debt of gratitude. For many people today the city and its cats are synonymous. Venice has its famous cats and its unknown cats, past and present. There are street cats and palace cats, and tourists come to see them as they come to see the gondolas, canals and glassworks.

Today, 12,000 cats still look after the city of the Doges, which only has 80,000 inhabitants. A society has been set up to protect, feed and vaccinate the cats and control their numbers by neutering. The city is currently working on providing a refuge for them – after so many years they have certainly earned it.

It was decided to fetch whole boatloads of cats from the east, where they had the reputation of being particularly savage hunters.

The cats were released into the streets and the rats took refuge in the canals, which marked the beginning of the end of the plague.

# CLEVER CATS

A cat, they say, always lands on its feet. It certainly has an extraordinary sense of balance, and an astonishingly supple body which enables it to right itself with the most amazing contortions. It has a spine with tiny discs that separate the vertebrae, which makes it extremely mobile, and they also act as shock absorbers. If a cat falls backwards it immediately twists its head round, and then rotates the whole body. Thanks to its eyes and an "internal ear," a vestibular appliance, it is able to "picture" its line of fall. The muscles immediately obey the orders of the brain. The cat, once facing the ground, breaks its fall by extending its front legs and flexing the back ones several times to keep its balance.

It is not a good idea to deliberately drop a cat to see what happens however; surprised or cross it could make a mistake and easily crack its skull. And if a cat falls from too high a drop it can hit the ground too hard.

Many circus acts include performing dogs which, poor things, are more or less willingly dressed up and taught to do tricks to amuse us. Cats are hardly ever used for the same sort of act, but in the Moscow Circus there is a clown who works with cats that really do seem to enjoy the performance as much as he does. How does Yuri get good results night after night? He explains that his act consists of three tricks, and in fact he teaches three different cats the same trick, so with nine cats there are always two in reserve for each trick, and if one does not cooperate every time, out of the three he is certain to have one cat that will work!

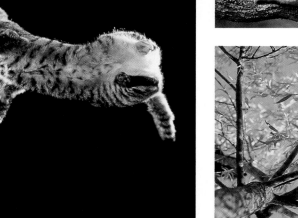

# OWNED BY A CAT

O ver the last hundred years the cat has seen its way of life change radically. Pedigree cats in particular have become the pampered and cloistered representatives of their breed. Leading a more restricted and disciplined life, the show cat, if it is successful at winning medals, becomes a marketable commodity, representing financial gain.

The object of daily care and grooming, its diet strictly supervised and living in more or less restricted surroundings, there will be no unexpected romantic encounters for this cat. Its love life will be strictly supervised! Except if a breeder is trying to create a new variety by crossing, the pedigree cat will only ever mate with one of exactly the same antecedents. The poor old tom cat on the roof who hears some beautiful Persian or Birman lady calling from her golden prison will be out of luck!

Has the cat then totally changed now that it no longer has to worry about finding food and shelter and is pampered and cosseted? No – it remains what it has always been: an apparently domesticated animal whose love for its owner is such that it has to be returned.

The cat chooses its owner. Whatever the breed, they all exhibit the same attachment, some more openly than others but all to the same degree. From the Chartreuse, the "dog in a cat suit," to the Chinchilla who follows you around "talking," to the Siamese who is capable of letting itself die if separated from its owner, to the non-pedigree who seems to understand the slightest gesture made to it, all remain faithful to the choice they have made. While happy to be part of a family and a friend to all in it, there is usually one person who is their favourite and can do anything with them. But the right has to be earned by respecting the cat's freedom, unlike the case of the elderly lady who spoiled her black and white moggy shamelessly and could never understand why the claws came out and the cat rejected her when she pestered it with too much petting.

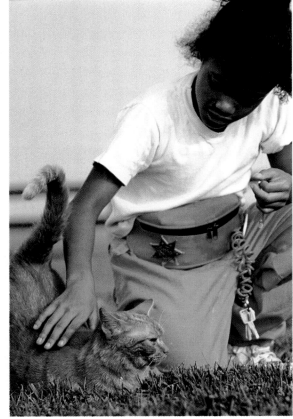

# CATS AND OTHER ANIMALS

"They fight like cat and dog ...." Everybody knows the expression, which must have been invented by someone who knew nothing of cats. If ever there was an untrue saying this is it. Though, of course, we all know of unpleasant people who think it amusing to encourage their dog, usually a big, fierce one, to chase cats.

Statistics prove the saying to be nonsense: in Europe more than half the people who keep dogs keep a cat too. And the two animals get on wonderfully.

If a cat does not feel threatened it can prove the best of companions for the most unlikely of animals, and there are innumerable cases of cats befriending creatures which it would have absolutely no intercourse with in the normal course of events. Horses, in particular, accept a feline companion and sometimes seek one out. Racegoers know the famous story of the thoroughbred who would never go to the course without his magnificent black tomcat friend. The cat, seated on the horse's rump, would patiently wait for the races to finish and then go back to the stable which he shared with his friend.

There is a moving story of a chick whose mother had been killed by a car soon after its birth and which was adopted by a Danish cat called Pully. Pully picked the chick up carefully in her mouth and took it to her own straw bed. An exemplary mother, the cat helped the chick to find food, protected it from the other hens when the farmer's wife strewed grain for them, and held it between her paws while it slept. When the chick grew up it integrated with the other hens but never forgot who had cared for it, and the cat and the hen could be seen walking around together, the cat quite calmly and the chicken preening itself!

On another farm a female cat called Fandora happily suckled both Prissy, her own kitten, and Figaro, a fox cub which the farmer had found abandoned.

# THE CAT ASLEEP

It is said that the cat sleeps with one eye open. In fact cats have two levels of sleep: a deep sleep, in which it is totally lost to the world, and a shallower level in which it probably dreams.

The cat spends more time sleeping than any other family pet. Attempts to analyse the cat's sleeping pattern have revealed that on average it sleeps about six hours a night with one hour of shallow sleep. This is characterised by involuntary movements: whiskers that suddenly tremble, paws and tail that twitch nervously and fur that stands on end. Flickering eyelids and sudden shifts in position are also typical of this sleep level as are faint miaows – all of which make the cat look as though it is dreaming.

Whilst the cat sleeps a lot it is not always a peaceful sleep. Depending on the individual or type of cat, the sleep pattern may be more or less turbulent according to the time of day or night, the place in which the cat has chosen to curl up, or the state of its digestion.

The adult cat on average also spends the equivalent of fifty percent of its day in shallow sleep, fifteen percent in deep sleep and only thirty-five percent wide awake.

Even if a cat changes its circumstances it will not change its sleeping pattern. More sensible than people, if it is suddenly given more freedom it will not make up for lost time gallivanting out on the tiles, it will sleep as usual when it needs to sleep.

Sometimes when a cat wakes up it will lie for a few seconds with its eyes open but looking as if it were still in some dream. Can cats really dream? No one knows the answer. They appear to be dreaming in shallow sleep, and those involuntary movements make it look as if they are chasing some prey in a dream, but this is probably a misinterpretation of a purely mechanical, physical reaction.

However, when a cat really sleeps badly and wakes up too suddenly, the reason is quite clear: a healthy cat sleeps well and at its own usual times. If it is sleeping badly it is a good idea to get the vet to look at your cat.

# THE CAT AT PLAY

From the moment it opens its eyes and moves away from its mother, the kitten begins to play. It teases its brothers and sisters, pushes and chases them and looks absolutely enchanting as it does so. Mother cat keeps an eye on them but only intervenes if she thinks the game is getting too rowdy. She knows that the leaping and chasing and mock fighting builds up the kitten's strength, resistance and liveliness. And as the kitten grows, even when it is alone, it will still play. It tries to catch everything that moves within its reach: the feather carried by a draught, a cork dancing on the end of a piece of string or a rolling ball, and it also chases insects and later on mice ....

Much has been written about the cruelty of the cat. But the truth is that the cat, as it catches the mouse and then pretends to let it go, only to catch it again, is simply playing a game. The prey has become a live cork on a string or a ball that runs instead of rolling.

Observers of the cat believe that the movement of anything small that slides, rolls, or above all runs away, triggers off an automatic series of coherent movements in response.

One only has to look at the face of a cat playing with a mouse – who can honestly say there is the least hint of cruelty in its eyes?

# GROOMING

The cat is a clean animal. You only have to watch it washing itself to be assured of the fact. The activity of washing is an instinct and often goes beyond mere cleanliness. It is also a way for the cat to cool itself, get rid of sweat and eliminate any dead hairs or other impurities that may be caught in its fur. And by using its teeth and claws it also gets rid of parasites. In addition, by licking itself the cat imbibes small quantities of vitamin D which the sun has produced on its coat. The mother cat teaches her kittens to wash. From birth she licks them often and for a long time, and so teaches them to be clean. Amusingly, kittens pick up the idea quickly and are soon licking each other and mum, too.

The cat cleans itself at every opportunity. It performs extraordinary contortions to reach the apparently-inaccessible parts of its body. It is equipped with the perfect tools for the job: a rough tongue which works like a brush, claws and teeth and even the pads of its feet, with which it rubs the damp fur.

But it cannot reach absolutely every part. The inside of the ear, for instance, the nostrils, the teeth and the anal gland are inaccessible and the cat needs your help to clean these. This should be done gently and slowly since cats hate rough treatment.

For a shorthaired cat a firm but gentle brush over in the direction of the hair, once or twice a week will suffice. A damp wool rag rubbed over the coat will keep it glossy. Longhaired cats need more complicated grooming. They need brushing and combing out against the lie of the hair and a flea comb should be used regularly on them to get rid of any parasites or bits of garden debris picked up in the fur, and also to prevent knotting. This should be followed by a final brush over.

Cats can be bathed but only very occasionally, otherwise the natural oils in the coat will be destroyed. The water should be tepid and the head kept out of the bath. The cat should be rinsed and immediately and thoroughly dried.

Once a week the eyes, nose, ears, mouth and anal gland should be checked.

# A NATURAL HUNTER

Whether taught by its mother or left to fend for itself when very young, the cat quickly discovers the trick of catching its prey. The exercise is carefully planned. First the cat locates its victim. It knows the places the mouse or other creature frequents and, moving downwind of it creeps up, ears pricked. Suddenly the cat is seized by an almost imperceptible trembling. The rear end twitches from side to side, while it seems to dig its claws into the ground. It judges the distance by sight and suddenly it bounds. The back legs provide the motive force for the leap while the front are left free to grab its victim. It gives its prey a bite on the nape of the neck, between the vertebrae, to kill it quickly if not instantaneously. If the prey is large – a rat for instance – the cat will fight to the end and not back off.

The cat was born to hunt. It is an instinct which still survives when it no longer has to hunt to eat. Without it the cat would not have survived in the wild. And even today we have invented no better method of exterminating rodents than the services of a cat.

The cats does not kill for pleasure – it kills because it knows that that is its job.

# CATS, WATER AND SNOW

Generally speaking, cats do not like water. They hate being bathed and get used to it with difficulty. The cat really has to be escaping in danger of its life before it will jump into a lake or stream of its own accord. Strangely, though, if a cat does end up in the water for the first time, it instinctively knows how to swim and will get out alright – as long as it does not have to swim too far, since it soon runs out of breath.

Many cats will have nothing to do with the water even though they have realised they can survive in it. A few, on the other hand, love it and will dive in.

Of the pure bred cats there is only breed which is known to be totally happy in the water: the Lake Van cat from Turkey. But no one knows why they are the exception to the rule.

But while cats do not like water they have no problems with snow. Seeing snow for the first time they will timidly proceed, one paw at a time. They soon realise the strange white blanket on the ground is not dangerous, even if it is rather cold. You can see young cats playing and rolling in the snow – until their fur gets wet!

# CATS AND KITTENS

It is an undisputed fact that cats love their kittens. From the moment of birth the mother cat watches over them, knowing they are weak and blind. When, eight days later, they open their eyes to the world she hardly leaves them for a second except to eat, and even then keeps one eye on them.

Anxious and ready to spit at any stranger who comes near, she is a living wall between them and the world. And when her little ones start to move and play she redoubles her watchfulness.

The mother cat is a born teacher. The first thing she teaches her kittens is how to play. This is an important part of their physical development, building muscles and improving reflexes and also teaching them, as they chase each other's tails, the skills they will need later for hunting.

Hunting is a primordial occupation for cats who live in freedom, in the country for instance. But the role of the mother cat is much reduced for those pedigree animals who have to live in towns, perhaps in an apartment. When the mother cat and her kittens have access to barns and cellars and trees she really comes into her own. Through her, the kittens learn to creep up on things, to move silently and freeze into immobility, or move swiftly along the ground.

The mother cat will bring her kittens pieces of dead prey, and later on whole dead mice. Finally she will bring back living prey, teaching her kittens that when she lets it go they have to retrieve it and kill it. This is not cruelty, it is a simple lesson in survival.

Occasionally the model mother apparently behaves curiously out of character. Some cats kill and eat one or several of their kittens. This, happily very rare, occurrence is thought to be due either to thyroid problems in the mother cat, or more simply that she has insufficient milk to feed them or – and this seems the most likely given the cat's concern for her offspring – the fact that the mother knows the kittens are unhealthy or deformed in

some way not necessarily apparent to us. By sacrificing them at birth she saves them from a miserable life and by eating them removes all trace of her action.

It is known that rats practice this kind of population control, so why not cats, too?

# FREEDOM AND ...

The cat can change quite radically when on its own, particularly if it thinks no one is watching. It reminds one of the badger, nicknamed the clown of the night, as it pursues ends known only to itself. Constantly watchful, reacting to the slightest sound, the cat explores the terrain inch by inch, even if it knows it well already, for the cat believes things may have changed since it was last there and it is right. Under the cat's nose is a new, unknown insect, the wind has covered the ground in dead leaves and the rain has made new grass grow.

Almost silent in the house, the cat can become noisy in the open air: calling to a female in season or merely letting other cats know he is there on his territory (the cat sprays the four corners of its territory like a dog, to mark it against intruders). Or it may also be warning or offering to fight some other imprudent creature. The noise then turns into a menacing growl, it snarls and shows its teeth and the ears either prick up or flatten against the head. And sometimes the cat will choose a tall tree from which it can keep a look out and spring on the unwanted visitor.

Out of doors everything interests the cat. Up on its hind legs it tries to catch anything that flies by – maybe a butterfly or just a feather fallen from a bird.

If it is feeling safe, it will take the opportunity to really stretch out on the ground and have a sleep. In the house there is not always a huge bed available, and a cushion has its limitations after all!

There are friends to be met outside, too: the next door cat for instance is an accepted pal and there are trees to sharpen the claws on. The cat knows what happens if it tries doing that to the furniture!

And perhaps the proud alley cat pities the Persian, a prisoner of its own beautiful coat, or the Abyssinian, victim of its own beauty, the Chartreuse dreaming of impossible forays, or the American Curl who, in the outside world, might be ashamed of its strange ears ....

To be a house cat, with guaranteed board and lodging, meals served on a plate and a clean bed to sleep in, has its attractions. But to be able to combine this life with hours of liberty – what more could a cat ask?

# ... CURIOSITY

**E**ven if a cat is not able to go out and about it will explore the house it lives in.

Cats are into everything. A houseplant is an excuse to play with the leaves, an empty jar may still retain a delicious smell, an open box is an invitation to climb in. Cats love to edge their way into exciting places. The linen cupboard door left open is just an encouragement to curl up on the clean sheets. A hat box becomes a hiding place and some string or a necklace can be great fun to get tied up in.

But it is not all playfulness; the cat explores as much out of a need to know. After all, there may be some nasty surprises in store. It is best to be sure, and the nose, whiskers and paws are all used in approaching the strange object. You can't be too careful.

Cats often like music and the composer Scarlatti claimed that his Cat Sonata was literally dictated by his cat touching the harpsichord keys with its paws.

Everything new which comes within the cat's orbit has to be examined, on the outside and, if possible, the inside.

Having checked that all is well, does the cat then feel it can relax and wait for its owner to come home?

Who knows what goes on in the mind of the cat?

# GLOSSARY

**AGOUTI:** coat pattern with banded hairs of brown, black and yellow as found in wild feline species.

**BASTET:** ancient Egyptian goddess of fertility, portrayed with the head of a cat and the body of a woman.

**BLAZE:** a distinctive contrasting marking running down from the cat's forehead to the nose.

**BLUE:** colour of fur which may be any shade of grey from pale bluish grey to dark slate.

**BRITISH:** in addition to being the name of a breed (British Shorthair) it also denotes a stocky type of cat as distinct from one that is long and elegant.

**CALICO:** American name for a tortoisehell and white cat.

**CATNIP:** plant whose scent is irresistably attractive to cats. Also known as catmint

**CLASSIC:** name given in America to the most usual of tabby patterns, known in Britiain as "marbled".

**FERAL CAT:** wild cat.

**FOREIGN:** term used to describe cats which are the opposite of the stocky British type, specifically with the elegant outine and fine bones of the Siamese.

**FURBALL:** fur swallowed by a cat when washing which balls up into a sausage shape.

**GENETICS:** the study of heredity.

**GLOVES:** contrasting white feet.

**KINK:** a bend or twist in the tail caused by a malformation, thickening or break of two vertebrae. Once considered correct in the Siamese, it is now disliked.

**MASK:** area of the face when of a contrasting colour to the body.

**MUZZLE:** projecting nose and jaws of a cat.

**POINTS:** extremities of the body, head, ears, feet and tail which in certain breeds are coloured differently from the main colour of the cat.

**QUEEN:** female cat used for breeding.

**SMOKE:** term used to describe a cat whose undercoat is as white as possible with a black (or other colour e.g.blue) top coat which shades to silver on the sides and flanks. The undercoat shows through when the cat is in motion, giving a "smoky" effect.

**STANDARD:** the characteristics required for a recognised breed and by which cats are judged.

**TABBY:** name given to a cat with definite markings in bands, stripes or flecks. Said to be derived from a similarly patterned material first made in the Attabiy quarter in old Baghdad.

**TICKING:** term for the colour banding on each hair as seen on the Abyssinian.

**TIPPING:** contrasting colouring at the ends of the hairs as seen on the Chinchilla

**TOMCAT:** uncastrated male cat.

# INDEX

# PICTURE CREDITS

The photographs in this book, are drawn from from the files of the COGIS picture agency, and were taken by the following photographers: Annette Amblin, Bernard Bernie, Philippe Garguil, Jean-Claude Gissey, Jean-Michel Labat, Gérard Lacz, Yves Lanceau, Sylvie Lepage, François Nicaise, Hervé Nicolle, Gérald Potier, Rémy, François Varin, Serge Vedie, Frank Vidal, Paola Visintini. Picture page 124 by Kitamura/Gamma.

Produced by Copyright Studio, Paris
Design: Jacqueline Leymarie
Layout: Mireille Palicot
Picture Research: Martine Perrin-Jacquet
with the kind assistance of Pascale Renambot of the Cogis agency
English translation by arrangement with
Bookdeals Translations, P.O. Box 263, Taunton TA3 6RH